ELIMINATE NEGATIVE THOUGHTS: A practical guide on how to eliminate negative thoughts

James John

Table of Contents

Chapter 1

Clear your mind of negative thoughts

Being human means having negative thoughts from time to time, and fighting negativity can be difficult. This is the reason why you can find yourself wondering how to stop having bad thoughts all the time. You might be shocked to learn that the solution to this query is considerably more straightforward than it first appears to be.

The steady barrage of unfavorable thoughts that appear reasonable can easily drown even the simplest things. What would you do if you were able to ignore that roar?

Make new friends or try a different line of work? You don't have an overactive negative thought process, that much is true.

Our minds are constantly ready to speak negatively. Here are some explanations of why negative thoughts are so harmful and suggestions for dealing with them.

13 Techniques for Eliminating Negative Thoughts
Check out these tried-and-true methods for kicking bad ideas to the curb.

1.Determine the Triggers
Start to seek patterns in these spirals as you learn to monitor your thoughts objectively. Is there a typical trigger that sets off this spiral? Don't stop there after recognizing that, either.

Investigate more to discover the triggers and underlying feelings. What specifically about the trigger is having such a big impact on you? Are there still problems there that need to be resolved? Try to address the underlying cause rather than just the symptoms.

If it is too emotionally taxing, consult a therapist to resolve them jointly. In the long term, mending those open wounds or bruised scars beneath might assist in ending these spirals.

2. Read It Out
Celebrities tend to read their critical social media messages aloud, which makes you realize how stupid and ridiculous they are. Test it out while listening to your inner critic. Make a call to a buddy, tell them your bad ideas, and then chuckle at how absurd the mind can be.

It will be simpler for you to let go of the negative thinking and replace it with something positive if you utter these words because doing so will transform the energy around it. How this advice on how to deal with negative thoughts might affect your life will astound you.

3. Relate a Humorous Story or Joke
Laughter always shifts your perspective for the better. Laugh, tell a joke, or recall a humorous experience. Being funny with yourself is also never a negative thing! Laughter is a great passion that improves your life since it makes you happier and healthier. It does wonders for the soul.

Keep in mind that you can always use this advice to fend off negative thoughts when you notice them beginning to creep in. Of course, that doesn't imply you need to joke around all the time. It only implies that the best method for overcoming bad thoughts is to engage in an activity that makes you grin or laugh.

4. Retaliate

negative ideas, such as taking leadership. Do as I do when it tries to take over. Say "thanks for sharing" to it in your head and get on with your day. Fighting it won't help because it will only make the noise louder. Just reply to it and keep going!

It requires effort to implement this advice. Catch yourself if you notice any negative ideas beginning to enter your head. This awareness will make sure you can respond and change that thought. For instance, take a deep breath and glance in the mirror if you put on a dress and begin to feel self-conscious. Remind yourself that you are confident and you look wonderful rather than demeaning yourself.

5. Inhale
Take three long breaths to quiet your mind. Put an end to what you're doing, plant your feet firmly on the ground, and take a deep breath. Keep your distance, take a few deep breaths, and consider your next step.

The intellect benefits much from breathing. It is an essential component of meditation because of this. Feel your body fill up with oxygen as you inhale and exhale, from your nose to your lungs. You can also practice breath-based meditation by counting your inhalations and exhalations out loud so that you can concentrate on them rather than your distracting thoughts.

Simply being aware is the key to using breathing as a type of meditation. See if you can feel your body starting to relax after using this advice.

6. Set a deadline.

Negative thoughts won't go away by hanging out with you. Tell yourself that you will give such thoughts a maximum of one minute before rejecting them. Use the timer feature on your smartphone as an extra motivator. Don't let any unfavorable ideas resurface once it has gone off.

Even beginners can simply follow this practical advice on how to stop thinking negatively. After all, if a negative notion begins to seep in, it won't just go away.

You can be aware of your unfavorable thoughts and get ready for them by counting down. Although you can't completely "switch off" your mind, you may slow it down to a manageable speed by putting an end to pointless chatter.

7. Workout

Your mood will improve with exercise, as demonstrated by the current increase in group fitness mind/body classes. This makes it one of the most crucial methods for getting rid of bad ideas.

Smart exercisers have been doing this for years by participating in IntenSati, a breakthrough mind-body workout that teaches you to say happy words and apply the intents you learn in class to your daily life. One popular phrase spoken aloud in class is, "All negative thoughts stop right now!"

You may change your exercise from being a pointless job to something that is not only life-affirming but also healthy for your mind and body by using workouts like IntenSati.

Your cognitive and psychosocial function can even be improved by using this exercise method.

Additionally, it can work wonders for your self-esteem and eventually help you see the value of leading a life you love.

8. Modify Your Setting
It's not simple to learn how to stop thinking bad things. However, a change of scenery or even just leaving the room you're in might spur fresh cognitive processes.

Get up, leave the area, and shift your attention to something else. Laundry folding could be seen in a completely different and more advantageous way.

For instance, if you are sitting in your room and you notice that your mind is beginning to think unfavorable things, walk outside and open a window. You can stroll through your community if you want to go the extra mile. You'll gain access to fresh opportunities if you do this to change your emphasis.

Utilizing this advice might potentially change the way you perceive laundry folding for the better.

9. Record it.
Get those thoughts out of your head because negativity destroys positivity. Write down all of your concerns and set a timer for 5 to 10 minutes. Once you've finished, rip the paper into pieces and toss the list in the trash. Move on after clearing your throat.

Writing helps us think more logically and rationally while also allowing us to express our problems. It offers you the possibility to view yourself differently and acquire some kind of authority. This is especially useful when you're finding it difficult to advance with something.

Utilize affirmations.
Do you wish to learn how to quit worrying? When a bad thought pops into your head, have a positive response ready to speak to yourself. For instance, "Yes, I can, I can do it, and I'm working it out now." Find one that resonates with you and keep it nearby to silence the critical voice.

It is not required to be a complete sentence. Sometimes all it takes to explain what you want to tell yourself is a single word or a short phrase. Till you feel the bad thoughts leaving your mind, keep saying that out loud in your head.

Affirmations are a wonderful way to start the day on a happy and upbeat note before allowing any negative thoughts to enter your mind.

11. Employ a standard idiom

Enjoy yourself with this. When a bad thought pops into your head, respond with something amusing or entertaining. Smile, smack your wrist, or stick your tongue out. Find a physical reaction that will help you turn off your mind and refocus on the here and now. You can learn how to stop spinning by using this advice.

You can concentrate more on the response than the thought itself if you link your attempt to avoid bad thoughts with an activity. The accompanying negative notion merely recedes into the background.

If you want to see results from this approach, you must do it every day. The time spent practicing will be worthwhile.

12. Watch Without Prejudice
We are frequently our worst critics when the spiral of negative thinking begins. How stupid was I not to anticipate this? Why did I think this was ever conceivable? Where am I going wrong? "I keep doing the same things wrong," "Won't I ever realize what I did?"

Try shifting to the observer's position the next time you catch yourself thinking such unfavorable things while swimming in the deep end. Test your ability to soar above your thoughts and take a step back to observe. We frequently fail to see how our thoughts are absurd or absurd when we are too close to the circumstance.

Being an observer is similar to putting up a mirror in our minds to see how they are operating. This open, non-judgmental reflection enables us to recognize the errors in our assumptions. Moving ahead is made easier when we begin to see and understand the things that we were oblivious to when we were in the thick of things.

13. Quit evaluating yourself against others.
This is a crucial piece of advice for discovering how to stop thinking negatively. In the age of social media, it's quite simple to compare oneself to other people. According to a study, people become more depressed the more time they spend on Facebook.

People frequently post flattering photos and status updates that highlight their accomplishments. It's simple to judge yourself by the Facebook facade of your friends and find flaws. Then, you choose to share a status update that promotes you, and if it doesn't receive a ton of likes and comments, you might assume that your Facebook friends don't think highly of you.

The same holds for those who are in committed partnerships. They frequently act in this way because their peers have done the same. Observing someone's happy relationship status in the manufactured world of social media may be depressing if you're not in a fulfilling one. Without even realizing it, you compare yourself to them in the end.

Chapter 2

Manage your time and input

Chapter 3

Rewire your thoughts patterns

It's easy to slip into a downward spiral of negativity when life doesn't go as planned or feels out of control. Worst-case thoughts and what-if scenarios flood your mind. Worry and fear take over.

It is exhausting and unpleasant to fight against self-defeating thoughts all the time. And consider how that energy could be used more effectively to achieve goals, set new ones, or simply enjoy life. Negativity spirals can paralyze you even if you are not facing a serious hardship like a breakup, job loss, or health issue. Whatever the reason, your ability to thwart pessimistic influences will determine how happy you are.

End the negative cycle consciously. Negative thinking is a difficult habit to break, but if you stay AWARE, a straightforward mindfulness exercise that can assist you in rewiring negative thoughts to something more positive, you can stop the automatic cycle.

A Mindfulness Practice to Rewire Negative Thoughts is called AWARE.
ACCEPT
Stop when you notice that you are about to enter a dangerous area. Breathe in deeply. Sit calmly. Permit your emotions and thoughts to wash over you. You'll discover that they fluctuate, almost like the weather.

Keep in mind that emotions like fear, rage, and guilt are normal and fleeting. Ironically, allowing yourself to feel your supposedly unpleasant emotions lessens their power over you and their intensity.

WATCH
Be mindful of your body. What feelings come to mind? Perhaps you notice clenching of your teeth or pressure in your chest. In the areas where you are retaining tension, gradually relax.

Observe the inaccurate or cruel stories you tell yourself next. Your inner dialogue should be recorded. Do you see any recurring trends? Practice acting with curiosity and without judgment. Avoid categorizing your responses as "excellent" or "bad."

You can unplug from your reactions by taking on the position of an observer to assist you to gain perspective and distance from them. Making this space allows you to think and act more healthily.

ACT
Function with negativity rather than allowing it to derail your plans. Do this: To write in your journal for 15 to 30 minutes, set a timer. It's time to move once the timer goes off. Establish a to-do list. To restart the relationship, send a text to the date who bailed on you. You may choose your behavior going forward without having to be dictated by fear.

Imagining success. How will it appear when you accomplish your goal? What will it be like? No matter how much or how little progress you achieve, keep your attention on it and applaud it.

REPEAT

Repeat the previous three steps each time you notice yourself starting a downhill spiral: Accept, look, and do. Your good pattern becomes stronger the more often you do this.

EXPECT

Expecting realistic improvement is the last step in the AWARE framework. Don't be too hard on yourself. A shift in perspective doesn't happen overnight. Still, negative emotions will surface. That's alright! It's a chance because it provides you with more chances to practice your new habit. It will soon come naturally to you.

Create an emotional response strategy for yourself so that you are prepared for triggers.

You can better prepare yourself to deal with negativity when it occurs by expecting setbacks.

Your thoughts do not make you. I have 99 problems, 86 of which are entirely fictitious scenarios in my imagination that are causing me to worry for no discernible reason, as Bill Murray once quipped.

It serves as an excellent reminder that the majority of the unfavorable things you tell yourself never materialize. They might not even accurately reflect reality! Why focus on them so much? Instead, focus that effort on gaining more AWARENESS.

Chapter 4

Being more positive

It is possible to change your negative thoughts to positive ones. The procedure is straightforward, but it does require time and practice because, after all, you're forming a new habit. The strategies listed below can help you think and act in a more upbeat and cheerful manner:

Determine what needs to change. If you want to think more positively and be more optimistic, start by identifying the things in your life that you currently think badly about, such as your job, your commute, your plans, or a particular relationship. By concentrating on one subject, you can begin small and tackle it more constructively. Instead of thinking negatively to reduce your stress, try to think positively.

Examine yourself. Stop periodically throughout the day to assess your thoughts. Try to find a way to reframe your ideas if you notice that they are primarily negative.

Be amusing yourself. Give yourself permission to laugh or grin, especially when things are tough. Find humor in commonplace events. You feel less stressed when you can laugh at life.

Maintain a fit lifestyle. On the majority of days of the week, try to get in 30 minutes of exercise. During the day, you can also divide it into 5- or 10-minute intervals. Stress reduction and mood improvement are two benefits of exercise. Eat well to nourish both your body and mind. Get adequate rest. and acquire stress management skills.

Be in the company of uplifting individuals. Make sure the individuals you surround yourself with are upbeat, encouraging, and capable of providing insightful feedback. Negative people might make you feel more stressed out and make you doubt your capacity to handle stress in healthy ways.

Engage in constructive self-talk. Start by adhering to this straightforward principle: Don't speak to yourself in a way that you wouldn't speak to someone else. Be kind and supportive of yourself. When a negative thought arises, analyze it logically and counter it by focusing on your positive traits. Think of things you're glad for in your life.